To My Heart

Poetry

Itra

To My Heart
Poetry

ISBN: 9781958502259 (Paperback)

Homestead Albania Print
Haxhaj, Nd. 19
Bajze, Albania 4306
www.kimmalaj.com

First Edition: July 14, 2023

For my love.

Fluent expressions may not be my forte,
As a writer or poet, I may not portray,
But hear me say "I love you" with all sincerity,
From my heart, I speak a truth beyond disparity.

For eloquent verses may elude my grasp,
Yet love's language in my heart does clasp,
I know I love you, in a depth so profound,
Genuine and true, its essence resounds.

Words may stumble, fail to convey,
But love's truth remains, it won't sway,
From the depths of my heart, I'm sure it's real,
A love that's unwavering, I truly feel.

If you feel it,
You have to steal it,
Because it's that moment that makes your life.

I long for it, oh how I yearn,
To feel the sweetness of your lips return,
For my deepest desires, I fervently pray,
To have what I cherish, each and every day.

With every wish, my hopes take flight,
Yearning for fulfillment, with all my might,
I wish, I wish, for all that I adore,
And even more, forevermore.

Words of my heart for you, I express anew,
In search of understanding, my soul breaks through.
God, guide my steps to be what you desire,
Reveal to me the truth that fuels my inner fire.

I yearn to unravel the depths of my being,
To grasp the essence of my purpose, foreseeing.
Who am I in this vast, mysterious expanse?
Grant me clarity, Divine, in this intricate dance.

What am I, a vessel of untapped potential?
Unveil the layers that make my soul quintessential.
Show me the passions that reside deep within,
That I may discover the love that's always been.

Why do I walk this path, this journey of life?
Enlighten me, oh Lord, through struggle and strife.
For in the shadows of uncertainty, I seek,
To unearth the meaning of existence unique.

Though uncertainties surround me, doubts may arise,
I'll embrace the questions, searching with open eyes.
With faith as my compass, I'll find my way anew,
And share these words of my heart, dear friend, with
you.

I caught a glimpse of you, and love took hold,
Enchanted by your presence, my heart was bold.
I won your affection, a precious gift so true,
In your embrace, my love for you just grew.

But alas, our time together was too brief,
You departed, leaving me in sorrow and grief.
Now I'm left here, standing all alone,
Navigating life's journey on my own.

My eyes, they ache for the sight of your face,
No longer will my lips feel your sweet embrace.
Yet deep within my heart, love still resides,
For you, my paramour, it forever abides.

Wealth eludes me, the power, too,
Strength may waver, dreams askew.
But amidst all I lack, I find solace sincere,
For your presence, my love, is what I hold dear.

Money's allure may not grace my hand,
Yet in your presence, I forever stand.
No earthly power can match the love we share,
With you by my side, life becomes fair.

Strength may falter in life's demanding sway,
Yet your support fuels my resilience each day.
For with you near, I find courage anew,
Together, we face whatever life may pursue.

Material possessions may come and go,
But your presence, my love, outshines their glow.
In your embrace, I find all I truly need,
With you beside me, my heart is freed.

In the realm of dreams, no one compared,
To find someone like you, none had fared.
And when our paths finally crossed, it's true,
No thoughts arose, just being with you.

No grand plans formed within my mind,
In your presence, contentment I find.
For simply being by your side,
Fulfillment and joy, I cannot hide.

In the tapestry of dreams, you were unique,
A vision of love, so tender and meek.
And as reality merged with dreams so grand,
Being with you, my heart understands.

No need for actions, no need for schemes,
In your presence, my soul truly gleams.
For even in dreams, I longed for this view,
Just being, my love, just being with you.

Pray, explain why tears cascade without cease,
As love, once abundant, seems to decrease.
Their prayers seek peace, a tranquil release,
To dwell in your embrace, ne'er to cease.

In this world, where hearts ache and souls roam,
Grant us sanctuary, the place we call home.
Unite us with you, in eternal embrace,
Where serenity dwells, filling every space.

I yearn for you to be mine, my cherished love,
For my heart overflows, guided from above.
Since I witnessed you beside her, a tender start,
My love for you kindled, forever in my heart.

This flame shall not dwindle, nor its fire cease,
Bound by love's embrace, eternally at peace.
With each passing moment, our bond extends,
A love story unfolding, with no foreseeable end.

What does it matter if my love runs deep,
If forever with you, my heart wants to keep?
In my arms, a longing to hold you tight,
To be entwined, together, day and night.

How can it be, in this world so bright,
That without you here, my vision lacks light?
My heart aches, burdened by this pain,
Yearning for you, my love, yet in vain.

What does it matter if trials come our way,
If our love endures, unyielding, they say?
For in the depths of my being, I find,
A love that transcends all space and time.

Caring for you, the world I forsake,
In your embrace, love's fire awakes,
Not swayed by those who endlessly speak,
Their judgments hold no power, love's truth we keep.

A single "yes" from you is all I seek,
With love's bond, our souls will speak,
Unseen before, a life we'll weave,
Two celestial beings, love's grace conceived.

In your presence, love's spell I fell under,
For a time, you were absent, causing a ponder,
But with a song, I expressed my devotion,
Longing for your return, a heartfelt emotion.

You came back to me, embracing my plea,
Please, don't depart, leave me not alone and free,
Without you, my strength wanes, I can't endure,
Your absence dims the world, making it obscure.

How can I navigate this existence so drear,
When your eyes, the windows to your soul, disappear?
In this vast world, how can I truly live,
When your voice, a symphony, no longer gives?

Allow me to unveil the depth of my affection,
Though you already sense it, no need for correction,
Whenever you're held within my loving arms,
Our love transcends, defying life's harms.

Sunday holds a special place in my heart,
For on that day, we're never apart,
Though at times I may feel all alone,
In truth, you're with me, your presence shown.

You bring me joy, a happiness profound,
With you, I feel liberated, unbound,
In your embrace, I find a fantasy's delight,
That's why I believe you're always by my side.

You make me whole, my spirits rise,
In your love, I soar to endless skies,
Together, we create a world so grand,
A love that lingers, hand in hand.

Whenever "love" echoes in my ear,
A craving sensation does appear,
It feels as if it's slipped away,
Missing from my life, gone astray.

Yet deep within, a glimmer remains,
A flicker of hope that still sustains,
For love's elusive nature can deceive,
Perhaps it's near, waiting to be retrieved.

So, I'll keep listening for love's sweet sound,
In melodies and words, it may be found,
Though it may feel distant, I'll persist,
For love's embrace, I cannot resist.

You are so pretty,
That's why I'm calling you sweetie.
You are so fine,
but I don't know if I'm gonna make you mine.

When I missed my love,
I thought I died.
Then I thought of you
And I said yes, "I'm alive."

Content I am to exist,
Content I am to cease and desist,
I find joy in a heartfelt smile,
And embrace the tears, even for a while.

For those untouched by pain's harsh sting,
Love's true essence may remain a mysterious thing,
It is through trials and sorrows endured,
That love's depth and meaning are truly secured.

My love for you, a truth you know,
You are my life, my heart's sweet glow,
I can't imagine a world without your embrace,
When the sun fades, you're my guiding grace.

You shine like a radiant light, so bright,
The moon and stars pale in your sight,
Don't deny the love we share so true,
Don't say you're not mine, my love, don't misconstrue.

Yet, if you desire a different path to pursue,
I'll respect your wishes, my love, it's true.
But know that my heart will always be near,
Forever cherishing the love we held dear.

The depth of my love, I can't comprehend,
If I made you mine, our bond won't end,
With all my heart, I professed my love true,
But alas, you never awakened to the clue.

I yearned for a future filled with us,
But you rejected, denying the trust,
That's how it is, the world still remains,
I won't be alone, another love sustains.

A new flame ignites, another enters,
Our hearts entwined, destiny adventure,
Together we'll journey, never to part,
Creating a love that's boundless, heart to heart.

Longing for a companion, someone to hold,
Craving their presence, a need untold,
Love's flame burns within, fierce and true,
Yet nobody returns the affection I pursue.

Mysteries unfold, something stirs in the mist,
An enigma, a feeling, a subtle twist,
Uncertain of what transpires, where it leads,
I stand in curiosity, for clarity I plead.

You are my sole reason to embrace life's endeavor,
To marry and be with you, my heart's endeavor,
Let the moon and stars grace our sacred union,
Witnessing our first kiss, a love in communion.

Together, let's soar through the vast expanse,
Seeking the stars' memories, our love's chance,
Across the world, on wings we'll traverse,
Proclaiming our love, an eternal verse.

For what I feel for you defies all words,
A love beyond measure, as vast as the birds,
From the depths of my heart, this fervent flame,
Words cannot capture, yet love remains the same.

Reveal to me life's true essence, stripped of your disdain,
Mistakes are made by all, no perfection to attain,
Your absence won't hinder, I'll strive on my own,
Discovering my true self, seeds of growth sown.

I'll live life on my terms, liberated and free,
Rejecting your expectations, embracing authenticity,
No longer imprisoned by your restrictive gaze,
I'll honor the gift God bestowed, finding my own ways.

Though you may envision a path shrouded in despair,
My heart finds solace, for God's guidance is there,
Assisting me on my journey, leading me astray,
To a place of completeness, where perfection may lay.

Perhaps it may seem audacious, my aspirations vast,
But this path aligns with me, like a symphony that lasts,
It beckons me to venture forth, to find my own tune,
A harmonious melody, where my spirit finds its commune.

The immortal soul soars to heights unknown,
Love everlasting, our hearts tightly sewn,
Words spoken, deeds done, eternally alive,
Continuing their dance, they forever thrive.

I awaited your arrival, and here you are, my dear,
A beacon of light in the darkness, crystal clear,
Our paths converged, a serendipitous sight,
And now, nothing compares with you as my light.

Yet, if you love me deeply, I implore,
Grant forgiveness, for life held temptations galore,
Until our fateful meeting, my heart unfulfilled,
But now, you alone, my desires distilled.

In this vast world, nothing can compare,
To the love you embody, so precious and rare,
Oh, my sweet love, you're truly divine,
The epitome of desirability, forever mine.

Why I don't have a reason to live.
In times when life seems bleak and dim,
When reasons to carry on grow thin,
I question why I should continue to strive,
When purpose eludes, barely alive.

But amidst the shadows, a flicker remains,
A glimmer of hope that quietly sustains,
For even in darkness, seeds of hope can grow,
Unveiling reasons to live, as shadows bestow.

Though the path may be clouded, unclear,
There's solace in knowing that change is near,
In the depths of despair, new meaning may arise,
Transforming a life once desolate, into a vibrant prize.

So hold on tight, for storms can bring light,
Even when reasons to live are out of sight,
Embrace the journey, let hope be your guide,
Discovering new purpose, with each stride.

Gratitude fills my heart, like a gentle breeze,
For all the moments, both big and small, that please,
Thank you for the laughter, shared in joyful embrace,
And for the support, that lifts me with grace.

Your kindness, a gift that brightens each day,
The caring gestures that never go astray,
For lending an ear when my soul needed to speak,
Thank you for being there, in both strong and weak.

Through the highs and lows, you've stood by my side,
Offering comfort and love, a constant guide,
With each act of generosity, you touch my soul,
Thank you for everything, making me feel whole.

In the depths of my heart, tears cascade,
Yet within my soul, happiness is made,
But how long will this duality persist,
Until when shall this conflicting state persist?

When sorrow engulfs, my heart can't conceal,
Amidst the pain, my soul finds its zeal,
But as time moves on, I question the duration,
How long will this inner contradiction find
continuation?

With each tear shed, my spirit finds release,
Yet I yearn for harmony, a sense of inner peace,
Until when shall this dichotomy endure,
Resolving the conflict, finding a cure?

But amidst the paradox, I hold onto hope,
That one day, this turmoil will loosen its rope,
When my heart and soul align, in perfect symphony,
Finding solace, unity, and serenity.

You queried my love, seeking an explanation,
Yet it eludes words, defies simple narration,
For it resides in your heart, a knowledge so deep,
In your mind's realm, emotions truly seep.

If compelled to articulate, it would unfold,
The fragrance of your hair, an aroma so bold,
The captivating aroma that envelops your skin,
Drawing me closer, a desire from within.

Your eyes, so beautiful, hold a magical sway,
When they meet mine, I feel carried away,
Weightless, as if suspended in mid-air,
Your gaze elevates me, beyond any worldly affair.

The gentle rush of your breath, an enchanting sound,
Whisking me away, as my senses surround,
Powerless I stand, enthralled by your grace,
In your presence, nothing else can find a place.

So, you see, my love, it defies explanation,
An ineffable bond, beyond mere contemplation,
It dwells in our hearts, a connection that persists,
A love that thrives, where words cease to exist.

If the words are born from deep within,
From your heart's truth, where love does begin,
Then they hold the essence of what is real,
But if from the mind, caution may reveal.

For the heart speaks with an authentic voice,
While the mind can sometimes distort the choice,
So, listen closely to the beats of your heart,
And let genuine love guide every part.

Tears of joy from pain of love,
From the depths of love's tumultuous sea,
Tears of joy emerge, a dichotomy,
Born from the pain that once held sway,
They glisten with resilience, come what may.

Each drop tells a tale of a heart once broken,
A journey through emotions, words unspoken,
But as pain subsides, like a fleeting dove,
Tears of joy arise, a testament of love.

They cascade like rain, cleansing the soul,
Transforming wounds into stories untold,
For in the realm of love, where passions reside,
Tears of joy bloom, love's balm to provide.

They whisper of strength found amidst the strife,
Of hearts reborn, embracing a new life,
And within their shimmer, hope takes flight,
Healing wounds, illuminating love's light.

So let the tears of joy interweave,
With the pain of love, a tapestry they conceive,
For in their fusion, a symphony unfolds,
A testament to love's resilience, as it beholds.

If your love for me is profound and true,
As mine for you, a love that grew,
Express it, my baby, let it show,
Never, ever let me go.

Tell me, oh tell me, without a doubt,
That your love for me will never fade out,
With every breath, let your feelings flow,
Never, ever let me go.

In your words, let the affection reside,
With each vow, let our love collide,
Promise me, my love, let it echo,
Never, ever let me go.

I wonder, oh how I wonder,
If you ever think of me, let my presence ponder,
When the wind whispers, does my name drift by,
In the cold, do you sense my warmth nearby?

On your gloomiest days, do I bring a smile,
With words unspoken, just for a while,
As you gaze at the stars, do I linger in your sight,
I wonder, oh how I wonder, through day and night.

In the realms of your thoughts, do I find a place,
Or do I fade away, a mere fleeting trace,
These questions, they linger, like a curious spell,
I wonder, oh how I wonder, only time can tell.

I swear for the moon,
I swear for the sun,
I swear for the stars that you are the only one.

Within my heart's depths,
I sought a reason profound,
For my soul's existence,
But there, too, I found,

Trapped and burdened,
In the grip of despair,
Unable to break free,
From its relentless snare.

Don't think that I'm pretending,
Because my love that I have is just for you.
All the messages that I'm sending,
Don't they all say that I do.

Tears fall from the sun, as it mourns our divide,
Your departure has left me feeling hollow inside,
Sadness engulfs me, a heavy burden to bear,
The moon hides in darkness, unwilling to share.

Alone, without you, its glow refuses to show,
Concealing its face, unwilling to bestow,
But if you would only turn your eyes towards me,
The sun would smile, the moon would be set free.

In your gaze, their radiance would reclaim the night,
A harmonious dance, love's celestial light,
So, look upon me, and let the heavens align,
With your presence, the sun shall beam, the moon
shall shine.

It took hearts to break.
It took souls to shake.
Just to tell you,
How much I love you.

In our union, loneliness has no place,
For you are exquisite, full of grace,
Your heart intertwined with mine,
Our love eternal, a bond divine.

Like souls destined for heavenly heights,
Our love shall endure infinite nights,
Now here, together, you and I,
United for all eternity, our spirits shall fly.

A sorrowful ache envelopes my soul,
Longing for you to make me whole,
I search the surroundings with a hopeful eye,
Yet you're nowhere near, no matter how I try.

I questioned the sun, pleading for a clue,
"Have you seen my loved one? Is it true?"
The sun replied, "Their here with me, dear,
Can't you see? Their radiant rays are clear.

The light that shines upon you, my friend,
Is their love, from beginning to end,
Though physically apart, their presence prevails,
In every sunbeam, their affection unveils.

Within my dreams, I search with longing,
For the one with whom I wish belonging,
Prayers whispered, hoping for that day,
When distance dissipates, not far away.

They say our stories are predestined, etched in time,
But my life's tale commenced when you became mine,
From that fateful meeting, our paths aligned,
A narrative woven, uniquely designed.

To me, you're the sun, bringing radiant light,
Illuminating my days, chasing away the night,
You're the moon, casting a gentle glow,
Guiding me through darkness, a comforting show.

In my dreams, you reside, a cherished part,
I wish to remain within their realm, never to depart,
For you're the embodiment of my deepest desire,
A presence I long to keep, a love to never expire.

Oh, the wonders love could bring,
If it bestowed its gift upon my being,
I searched high and low, far and wide,
Yet, nothing came forth, no love to abide.

Just as I felt defeated and left behind,
Love arrived, its presence so kind,
Embracing the beauty of its serendipity,
Love revealed its magic, wonderfully.

You, a wish crafted upon a distant star,
A dream fulfilled, descending from afar,
Sent to me from the heavens above,
A manifestation of pure and boundless love.

A flower, adorned with nectar's delight,
Lips so sweet, a kiss's exquisite height,
Musk's fragrance, mist's gentle embrace,
I possessed it all, a dream once in place.

The taste savored, each moment embraced,
A cherished vision, my heart once embraced,
But alas, it faded, slipped from my grasp,
Leaving memories, a dream of the past.

By Arti Malaj

Northern Albanian Folk Tales, Myths and Legends

By Kim Malaj

Castle of Teskom

Recover or Yield

Protectors of Time

Guide Time Inside

Who Is Maggie

Twisting Hercules

My Mom Is an Alien

The Old Untold

By Itra

To My Heart